Stress and Nutrition

Health Media of America

Chairman

David Heber, MD, PhD, FACP
MD, Harvard Medical School
PhD, Physiology, University of California, Los Angeles
Chief, Division of Clinical Nutrition
University of California, Los Angeles School of Medicine

Vice-Chairman

Elizabeth Somer, MA, RD
BS Foods and Nutrition, Oregon State University,
MA Health Education, Ohio State University

Members

Margaret Edell, RD
BA Foods and Nutrition,
San Diego State University

Robert H. Garrison, Jr., MA, RPh
BS Pharmacy, University of Washington
MA Adult Education, San Diego State University

Laura Granger, MPH, RD
BS Foods and Nutrition,
University of California, Davis
MPH San Diego State University

Allison Hull, MPH, RD
BS Foods and Nutrition, University of Missouri
MPH University of Hawaii

Margaret McLaren, RD
BS Dietetics, State University College, Buffalo
BA Food Service Management
State University College, Buffalo

Wendy Shigenaga, RD
BA Dietetics, San Jose State University

Judith Swarth, MS, RD
BS Foods and Nutrition, Oregon State University
MS Health Education, University of Oregon

Stress and Nutrition
Judith Swarth, MS, RD

Publisher: Robert H. Garrison, Jr., MA, RPh

Editor In Chief: Elizabeth Somer, MA, RD

Managing Editor: Lisa M. Moye

Editorial Director: Janet L. Haley

Art Director: Scott Mayeda

Production Directors: Jeff Elkind, Irene Villa

Copy Editors: Norma Trost Foor, Jean Forsythe, Mary Houser,
Stephen C. Schneider, R. H. Garrison, Sr., RPh

Cover Design: Stefanko & Hetz, Jeff Elkind

Photography: Bob and Irene Nishihira, Carlsbad, CA

Illustration: Walter Stuart, Jennifer Hewitson

Copyright © 1986 by Health Media of America, Inc.

For information regarding volume purchase discounts contact:
Health Media of America, Inc.
11300 Sorrento Valley Road, Suite 250
San Diego, CA 92121

Printed in the United States of America.

ISBN 0-937325-03-1

Contents

Figure 1   Environmental Stressors

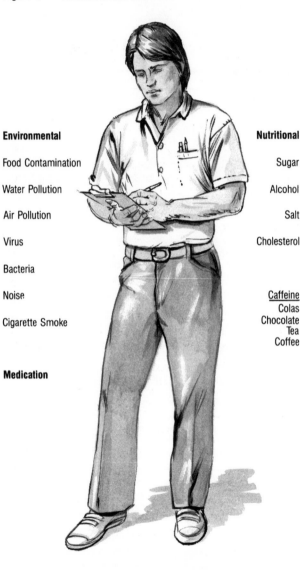

Environmental

Food Contamination

Water Pollution

Air Pollution

Virus

Bacteria

Noise

Cigarette Smoke

Medication

Nutritional

Sugar

Alcohol

Salt

Cholesterol

<u>Caffeine</u>
Colas
Chocolate
Tea
Coffee

1
What is Stress?

Stress is a part of life. Daily events bring challenges that tax the mind, body, and emotions. Individuals adapt to stress and learn to use it to their advantage. When stress is overwhelming, however, it can affect the quality of life.

People are subject to both physical and psychological stress. A cold day places physical stress on the body causing it to respond by changing circulation, breathing, and heart rate. Exposure to viruses, illness, and smoggy air all produce physical stress. *(Figure 1)* The pressure of a work deadline, the anxiety about a special social event, or the loss of a close friend are examples of psychological stress.

Stress is a force that pushes a person to change, grow, fight, adapt, or yield. All life events, even positive ones, cause some stress. For example, a promotion at work is a positive change, but the new job responsibilities can be stressful. Not all stress is harmful because the stimulation, challenge, and change might be beneficial to a person's life. For many people, however, there is too much stress and the ability to cope is strained. *(Table 1)*

Good nutrition is an important way to deal with the stress in life for three reasons:

1

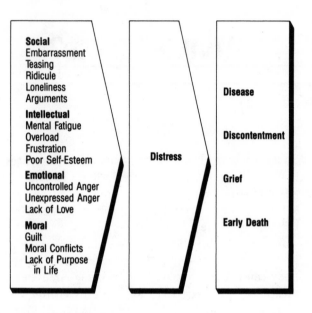

Table 1.   Psychological Stress

1. Nutrition affects how well an individual copes with the physical and mental demands of stress.
2. Poor nutrition causes stress to the body and mind.
3. Stress can increase the need for nutrients.[1]

The Stress Response

To understand why good nutrition is essential during periods of stress it is important to recognize how the body responds to stress. In a stressful situation, the body's built-in "fight or flight" response is triggered.

Epinephrine (adrenalin), the stress hormone, is released from the adrenal glands. This hormone, along with several others, travels through the body to increase blood pressure and heart rate, speed the breathing rate, and alter other body processses. Blood sugar also increases. The fat cells release fats into the bloodstream to increase available energy for the muscles. *(Figure 2)* The result of the stress response is an alert, aroused, tense state that prepares a person to meet danger. Once the stressful encounter is over, the body relaxes and returns to normal.[2]

Although physically dangerous situations are uncommon in modern society, some individuals react to stressful events in the same way as the caveman reacted to physical danger. Rather than running or fighting, however, a person holds the stress and can stay in a prolonged state of tension.[3]

Some stress in a person's life can be good, but problems result when there is too much stress. Stress-related disorders include heart disease, ulcers, allergies, asthma, rashes, hypertension (high blood pressure), and possibly cancer. Stress also can cause psychological problems such as depression, anxiety, apathy, eating disorders, and abuse of alcohol and drugs.

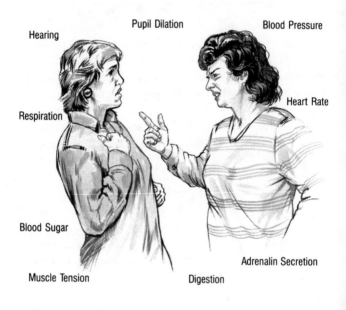

Figure 2. The Fight or Flight Response to Stress.

2
Stress and Nutrition

Poor nutritional habits can cause stress. Individuals increase the stress placed on the body by consuming too much sugar, caffeine, alcohol, sodium, and fat and too few nutrients.[4-6] Poor nutrition might upset the overall balance of nutrients and a poorly-nourished body is more susceptible to illness. Illness creates a greater need for nutrients within the body.[2,7]

For many people the irritations, frustrations, and environmental stress of daily life produce a state of chronic stress. Over the days, months, and years this can affect health. Nutritional needs also are influenced by the acute stress of infections, burns, wounds, surgery, broken bones, other illnesses and injuries, and sudden emotional upsets.[2,8] *(Table 2, page 6)*

Dietary Stress

Certain diet habits can create or add to stress in a person's life. These include caffeine, alcohol, sugar, and rigid dieting.[9-11]

Caffeine and Stress

The first cup of morning coffee provides a person with a boost to start the day. The boost is provided by

Table 2	Signs and Symptoms of Stress
Eye Strain	Headaches
Blushing	Teeth Grinding
Tight Neck & Shoulders	Jaw Clenching
Excessive Sweating	Rashes
Chest Pain	High Blood Pressure
Upset Stomach	Palpitations
Constipation	Shortness of Breath
Diarrhea	Cold, Clammy Hands
Nervous Tics	Curling Toes

caffeine. Caffeine stimulates the central nervous system and is found in tea, soft drinks, cocoa, chocolate, and some medications.

Caffeine is absorbed from the stomach and intestines and within minutes reaches the bloodstream and travels throughout the body. A person might feel more alert as mood is altered.

An excess of caffeine, however, can cause problems. Caffeine stimulates the stress hormones and heart beat and blood pressure can rise.[12,13] Both caffeine and the acids in coffee irritate the lining of the stomach and intestines. An overdose of caffeine might make a person feel agitated, anxious, restless, or dizzy. Sleep problems and headaches also might occur.

Drinking five or more cups of coffee a day can cause these symptoms.[12] Caffeine is a diuretic and causes increased urinary excretion of the B vitamins and vitamin C.[14] Caffeine can cause painful breast lumps, abnormal heart rhythms, and increased blood fats.[15] This stimulant also might increase the risk for cancers of the bladder, colon, and pancreas.[16-18]

A dose of 200 mg of caffeine, the amount in one to three cups of coffee depending on brewing strength, might cause undesireable side effects.[13] Older adults might feel the stressful effects of caffeine with fewer cups of coffee or tea than when they were younger.

Decaffeinated coffee is a good substitute for people who are suffering from stress. Other alternatives are instant coffee beverages that contain part roasted grains, or all-roasted grain beverages. Fruit juices, water, and herbal teas are also good substitutes for coffee. Check the ingredient labels of soft drinks and purchase those that are caffeine-free.

Sugar, Blood Sugar, and Stress

The consumption of sugar has increased.[19] One-fifth of the calories in the average American diet comes from refined sugar.[19] Although sugar is not an addictive substance, it has the potential to be abused. A diet high in sugar might be a substitute for more nutritious foods. Because sugary foods are easy to eat, excess calories are consumed and a person might become overweight.

Sugar is a carbohydrate and supplies energy. Several B vitamins are required to digest and process this energy, leaving less of the vitamins for other body processes. Thiamin, riboflavin, niacin, and vitamin B_6 are likely to be deficient in a high-sugar diet. For example, thiamin is essential for the function of the nervous system. A diet low in thiamin can cause fatigue, irritability, mental confusion, and depression.[20,21] All of these symptoms can increase feelings of stress.

Sugar also can add to mental and physical stress by its effects on blood sugar. A sugary food causes blood sugar to rise rapidly. To maintain equilibrium, the body releases a hormone from the pancreas called insulin. Insulin removes sugar from the blood and assists its uptake into cells. As a result, the level of sugar in the blood returns to a normal level.

Consuming a large quantity of sugar causes a rapid release of insulin. The sudden loss of sugar from the blood can leave the blood sugar level too low. Symptoms of low blood sugar include fatigue, hunger, headache, mental "cloudiness", blurred vision, trembling, nausea, anxiety, and perspiring. The mood swings and erratic behavior of some hyperactive children might be related to the effects of sugar on blood sugar.[22]

If a person consumes a concentrated sugar food and then experiences the unpleasant feelings of low blood sugar an hour later, he or she might be tempted to consume a sugary food again to appease feelings of hunger. This repeats the cycle. The periodic bouts with low blood sugar are stressful, and leave a person unprepared to cope with the demands and responsibilities of the day.

Caffeine also increases the rate at which sugar leaves the blood. This stimulant elicits a stress response itself and a cup of coffee with a sweet pastry is a very "stressful" way to start the day.

Whole grains and other unrefined carbohydrates contain chromium, a trace mineral that helps insulin regulate blood sugar.[23] A chromium-deficient diet has been linked to diabetes. Inadequate chromium intake is common in the American diet. It is estimated that as many as 90% of American diets do not supply sufficient amounts of this mineral.[24,25] Since excessive sugar increases blood sugar, but contributes none of the chromium needed for its entry into cells, additional stress is placed on the body to maintain blood sugar equilibrium.[24-27]

The United States Dietary Goals are guidelines for reducing the risk for the major degenerative diseases such as heart disease, hypertension, diabetes, and cancer, and related disorders such as obesity.[28] These guidelines recommend that sugar intake be reduced to no more than 10% of calories. *(Graph 1, page 10)*

Dieting: Friend or Foe?

Dieting can place stress on the body. A moderate decrease in calories is not a problem. When calories are drastically reduced, however, the body's equilibrium is threatened and a stress response might result.

The caloric level below which problems result varies and depends on body size, fat and muscle content, and metabolic rate. The metabolic rate is the total of body processes. Generally, a diet of less than 1,000 to 1,200 calories, or below 1,500 calories for a larger person, triggers a survival mechanism in the body.

When the survival mechanism is triggered, certain changes occur. The result of these changes is that muscle mass is lost, metabolism slows down, and the body burns calories at a much slower rate. Metabolism can decrease by as much as one-third.[29] At the same time, the percent of body fat increases. A per-

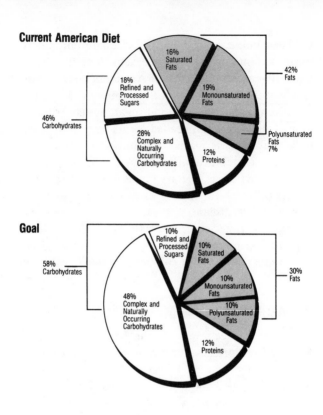

Current American Diet

16% Saturated Fats

18% Refined and Processed Sugars

19% Monounsaturated Fats

42% Fats

46% Carbohydrates

28% Complex and Naturally Occurring Carbohydrates

Polyunsaturated Fats 7%

12% Proteins

Goal

10% Refined and Processed Sugars

10% Saturated Fats

10% Monounsaturated Fats

30% Fats

58% Carbohydrates

48% Complex and Naturally Occurring Carbohydrates

10% Polyunsaturated Fats

12% Proteins

Graph 1. The U.S. Dietary Goals.

son can end a diet with a greater percent of body fat than when he or she started. Since fat requires fewer calories to be maintained, the body now needs fewer calories than before the diet. Returning to a normal food intake, the dieter now experiences weight gain on a calorie level that used to maintain weight. The weight regained is not lean muscle tissue, but might be as much as two-thirds fat. This is one explanation for the gradual increase in fat that is seen in people who have dieted frequently over the years.[29-31]

A low food intake and skipping meals can cause low blood sugar and its stressful syptoms. Nutrient deficiencies are common at intakes below 1,200 calories.[32] A lack of many nutrients can impair the immune system, the body's defense against infection and disease.[32,33]

Lack of success with weight control adds emotional and physical stress to the lives of millions of dieters. Dieters blame themselves for lack of will-power and suffer depression and anxiety over their inability to lose weight. Although obesity increases the risk for developing hypertension, cardiovascular disease, and diabetes, continually losing and regaining weight is apparently as stressful to physical health as the condition of overweight itself.[31,33-36]

Alcohol, Stress, and Nutrition

In times of stress, some people use alcohol to relax or escape. When alcohol is used to cope with stress it leads to abuse and alcoholism. Today, 95 million Americans obtain 10% to 20% of their caloric intake from alcohol. Alcohol has been called "the antinutrient nutrient" because it provides calories, but it does not provide vitamins or minerals. In addition to being an "empty calorie" food, alcohol depletes the body of several nutrients and creates additional needs for others.[37]

Unlike the other fuel nutrients (protein, carbohydrate, and fat) alcohol can be used as fuel only by liver cells. Normally the liver burns fat. When alcohol is present fat is not burned for energy but accumulates in the liver or is released into the blood. The result is an increase in potentially harmful fats circulating in the body, or possible liver damage.

Chronic, excessive alcohol consumption can increase blood pressure, damage the heart muscle, and can cause cirrhosis and alcoholic hepatitis. It also can increase the risk for cancers of the mouth, throat, and esophagus, and cause injury to the stomach and gastrointestinal lining. This latter condition can impair the body's ability to absorb nutrients and is one reason why heavy drinkers can become malnourished even if they are consuming a balanced diet.[37-40]

Since alcohol contains calories, weight gain is inevitable if a person continues to consume the usual amount of food. Nutrition suffers, however, if food intake is decreased to compensate for the calories in alcohol. Consumption of alcohol also produces a euphoria that decreases appetite and the desire for food. Although a glass of wine might stimulate the gastric flow and improve digestion, the irritant effect of excessive alcohol can reduce nutrient absorption.[37,38,40]

Alcohol metabolism requires a steady supply of B vitamins, particularly thiamin and niacin. These nutrients also are needed for cells to metabolize other foods for energy. When supplies of these B vitamins have been depleted by alcohol, blood sugar supplied by dietary sugars and starches can no longer be used efficiently and the result is low blood sugar, which is called hypoglycemia. This deprives all body tissues of energy.[41]

In chronic alcohol abuse, liver cells are unable to use vitamin D. Since vitamin D is needed for healthy bones and teeth and for the manufacture of several hormones, several body processes are affected by excess alcohol.[42]

Eyes also are affected by excessive alcohol use. The cells of the eye, which normally process vitamin A for use in vision, are busy processing alcohol and nightime eyesight suffers.[43]

One of the breakdown products of alcohol causes vitamin B_6 to be destroyed. This can result in anemia, fatigue, poor concentration, and lethargy.[44-46]

Alcohol is a diuretic and can dehydrate the cells of the body. Vitamins and minerals are lost with the water, including the B vitamins, vitamin C, magnesium, calcium, zinc, and potassium. The supply of folic acid (a B vitamin) to body tissues is also hampered by impaired absorption because alcohol interferes with the vitamin's metabolism.[39,40,43] A folic acid deficiency can result in anemia, lethargy, poor concentration, and weakness.[47]

Although a well-balanced diet and intake of nutrients might prevent severe nutrient deficiencies in the person who drinks and is affected by stress, the toxic effects of alcohol might affect the liver, heart, brain and other organs of the body. The risk remains of developing several diseases.[39,40,48,49]

Nutrition, Stress, and Immunity

The immune system defends the body against bacteria, viruses, radiation, chemicals, gases, and other environmental stressors.

The skin is also part of the immune system and forms a barrier against foreign microorganisms such as bacteria and viruses that could cause infection and disease.[50]

Evidence shows that stress might alter the immune system so it is unable to resist infection and disease.[51] Several stressors including lighting, noise, movement, and housing conditions hinder the immune system.[52-54] Although the initital response to a stressor might inhibit the body's defense system, the body can adapt if the stress is mild and prolonged.[55,56] *(Table 3)*

The loss of a loved one is the most stressful life event and is associated with an increased likelihood for illness and even death.[57] Although the stress response can vary between individuals, the loss of a loved one can reduce immune functions by as much as 50%.[51]

Depression alters immune function by reducing the amount of immune substances available to fight disease.[58,59] The degree of impairment might be related to the severity of the depression.[51]

The effect of stress on immunity is complex and probably combines several mechanisms including other hormones and body chemicals from the thyroid gland, sex glands, and brain.[51]

Behavioral changes are associated with stressful life events, including changes in sleep, exercise, drug use, and nutrition.[51] These changes also might affect immunity. Several nutrients are required for the immune system to operate effectively. A deficiency of protein or calories is a common cause of a depressed immune function.[33,50]

Table 3	What is Your Risk for Stress-Related Disease?			
Indicate how often each of the following applies to you in daily life.	3 Points Always or Usually	2 Points Some-times	1 Point Seldom	0 Point Never
Do you talk too fast?	_____	_____	_____	_____
Do you interrupt people or complete their sentences?	_____	_____	_____	_____
Do you hate to wait in line?	_____	_____	_____	_____
Are you short of time to get everything done?	_____	_____	_____	_____
Do you like to waste time?	_____	_____	_____	_____
Do you eat fast?	_____	_____	_____	_____
Do you often drive over the speed limit?	_____	_____	_____	_____
Do you do more than one thing at a time?	_____	_____	_____	_____
Do you become impatient if others do something too slowly?	_____	_____	_____	_____
Do you have little time to relax and enjoy the time of day?	_____	_____	_____	_____
Do you take on too many responsibilities?	_____	_____	_____	_____
Do you think about other things during conversations?	_____	_____	_____	_____
Do you walk fast?	_____	_____	_____	_____

(Continued on next page)

Table 3	**What is Your Risk for Stress-Related Disease?** *(Cont.)*			
Indicate how often each of the following applies to you in daily life.	**3 Points** Always or Usually	**2 Points** Some-times	**1 Point** Seldom	**0 Point** Never
Are you irritated when kept waiting?	____	____	____	____
Do you find that your fists are clenched or your neck or jaw muscles are tight?	____	____	____	____
Does your concentration often wander while you think about other responsibilities?	____	____	____	____
Are you competitive?	____	____	____	____
Your Total	____			

Score	Meaning
45-60	High Potential for Stress-Related Illness
35-44	Medium Potential for Stress-Related Illness
20-34	Low Potential for Stress-Related Illness

The young, the elderly, and those malnourished from illness or surgery are particularly susceptible to the problems of protein deficiency.[50] Simple infections might become life-threatening when there is a protein deficiency. Respiratory infections, diarrhea, hepatitis, tuberculosis, and other forms of severe infection might develop. There might be and increased vulnerability to minor infections and colds.[33,50,59-61]

Several vitamins and minerals might effect immunity. A deficiency of zinc, especially when there is protein-calorie malnutrition, causes destruction of tissues in the immune system.[33,61-63] Blood levels of zinc are likely to drop during infection.[62] Paradoxically, too much zinc, greater than 50 mg, alters copper status in the body and might depress immune response by impairing the ability of certain types of substances to destroy harmful bacteria.[64,65]

Inadequate intake of iron also impairs the immune system.[33,59] Women, children, the elderly, and persons with low incomes often consume too little iron in the diet.[66] The diet should include several iron-rich sources every day. (See page 25 for iron-rich foods.) *(Table 4)*

A deficiency of copper increases susceptiblity to bacteria and increases the risk for colds and infections.[33,67] Good dietary sources of this mineral include whole grain breads and cereals, shellfish, nuts, poultry, dried beans and peas, and dark green leafy vegetables. Copper should not be added to the diet as an individual dietary supplement without the advice of a physician.

Responses of the immune system are below normal without selenium. This is compounded if vitamin E is also deficient in the diet.[33,67] Selenium is found in meat, chicken, and fish and in whole grains and vegetables grown on selenium-rich soil. Vitamin E is found in nuts and seeds, vegetables oils (especially cold-pressed processed oils), and whole grain breads and cereals.

A deficiency of several B vitamins reduces immune function. Vitamin B_6 deficiency impairs immunity and increases the risk for disease and infection.[33,59] Folic acid deficiency impairs immunity. A deficiency of pantothenic acid, thiamin, riboflavin, niacin, and biotin also impairs immunity.[59]

Table 4	Food Factors That Affect Iron Absorption

Vitamin C: Vitamin C increases iron absorption. Consume vitamin C-rich foods with iron-rich foods.

Iron from animal sources: The iron in foods from animal sources (heme iron) is absorbed better than the iron from plant sources. When heme iron is consumed with foods from plant sources, the iron from plant sources is better absorbed.

Cast iron pots: Foods cooked in cast iron pots contains more iron than foods cooked in other cookware.

EDTA: Some food additives such as EDTA reduce iron absorption.

Eggs: Eggs reduce iron absorption.

Phosphorus: Phosphorus in diet soda, beer, and candy bars can interfere with iron absorption.

Calcium: Too much calcium in the diet can reduce iron absorption, unless iron intake also is increased.

The skin and mucous membranes that line the mouth, throat, eyes, and other body surfaces are a barrier to bacterial invasion and infection. Vitamin A is important in the maintenance of these tissues and a lack of the vitamin might increase susceptibility to disease.[68] In addition, immune cells that protect the body increase when there is adequate vitamin A.[33,69,70] Excess intake of vitamin A over 25,000 IU for adults, however, can cause toxic symptoms such as skin problems, vomiting, abdominal pain, hair loss, liver damage, and bone deformities.

There are indications that vitamin C status also affects immunity. Doses of vitamin C are able to reverse the suppressed immunity in animals[71] and the vitamin might reduce the frequency and severity of colds and infections.[72-75]

During times of stress, adequate dietary protein is important. The day's allotment of protein can be obtained from two servings of meat, chicken, or fish and two servings of low-fat dairy foods or several servings of whole grain breads and cereals combined with vegetables and dried beans and peas.

Antioxidants: Another Form Of Defense

Cell membranes are an important part of the body's defense against disease. They determine what compounds will and will not enter the cell.

Cell membranes are altered or damaged by free radicals, highly reactive compounds found in air, food, and cigarette smoke, or produced by radiation. Free radicals weaken the structure of cell membranes and encourage the development of several stress-related diseases such as cancer and cardiovascular disease.[76]

Antioxidants such as vitamin C, vitamin E, and selenium apparently protect cell membranes from destruction by free radicals.[77] Selenium is low in many diets and it is low in the blood of cancer patients, which has led to speculation that selenium deficiency relates to the risk of developing cancer.[78-82]

3
Environmental Stress and Nutrition

Polluted air, extremes of temperature, high altitude, and indoor lighting place stress on the body. The substances a person puts into his or her body, such as tobacco, medications and drugs, alcohol, and food, are also part of the body's "environment." Physical activity, though generally regarded as a positive force in our lives, can also cause stress.

Air Pollution

Living in areas with unclean air places physical stress on the body. Pollutants in air include oxidizing agents, such as ozone and nitrogen dioxide, that can damage the lining of the lungs. Ozone, for example, causes damage to the fats that make up the structure of cell membranes. Once damaged, the membrane no longer serves as an adequate barrier to harmful substances. The amount of harmful substances in the lungs increases during exercise in polluted areas as more air is inhaled and exhaled. When supplements of vitamin E are taken the amount of harmful compounds in the lungs is reduced. This indicates that the antioxidant effect of vitamin E neutralizes the highly reactive oxidizing agents in polluted air and protects the lungs from damage.[83]

Cigarette Smoking

Smoking one-and-one-half packs of cigarettes a day can reduce vitamin C levels in the body by as much as 30% to 40%. Smoking increases daily needs of vitamin C from 60 mg, the Recommended Dietary Allowance (RDA), to at least 100 mg.[84] Other estimates place the need at closer to 250 mg.[85] An 8 ounce glass of orange juice contains approximately 100 mg of vitamin C.

The stressful effects of cigarette smoke deprive body tissues of oxygen and are primary risk factors for the development of cardiovascular disease.[86] Smoking combined with caffeine might increase blood levels of cholesterol and increase the risk for heart disease.[15]

Temperature

Clothing and shelter are the major defenses against extremes of temperature. Changes in temperature might influence nutrient requirements. In normal temperature ranges the body controls heat loss and gain by constricting and expanding blood vessels in the skin to reduce or increase blood flow and, therefore, heat loss. The body also controls heat loss and gain by changes in the amount of perspiration produced.

In a hot environment, perspiration increases to lower internal body heat. Profuse perspiring results in a loss of water, sodium, potassium, and nitrogen. It also results, to a lesser extent, in a loss of iron, calcium, and magnesium. Needs for vitamin C increase in hot temperatures and needs for pantothenic acid, a B vitamin, might decrease.[87,88]

Exercise

Physical exercise is related to stress in two ways. First, it alleviates the physical and mental tensions and physiological changes that accompany stress. Secondly, exercise itself is a stressor on the body, changing patterns of nutrient use and creating a greater demand for certain nutrients.

The body does not respond to most psychological stressors with the "fight or flight" response. Therefore, stressful feelings and physiological stress products accumulate. Vigorous exercise is a means of "using up" these stress products. Instead of retaining a chronic level of stress in the body these potentially harmful substances are released. When the exercise ceases, the body is ready to return to a normal state of relaxation. In addition, exercise might redirect thoughts and attention away from the stress and leave an individual feeling mentally and physically relaxed.

Exercise prevents the build-up of chronic psychological stress, which is a risk factor for high blood pressure and heart disease.[89] Exercise causes healthful physiological changes in the heart and circulatory system. Circulation throughout the body is increased and the heart becomes stronger and beats less often to pump blood. Oxygen and nutrients reach body cells and waste products are carried away efficiently.

Elasticity of the lungs increases so that more air is taken in with each breath. Greater amounts of oxygen reach body cells and might delay the degenerative changes of aging. Risk of heart disease is also decreased as levels of harmful blood fats and cholesterol are reduced. The increased burning of calories from exercise helps control excess body fat, which is also a risk factor for developing heart disease and for the complications of diabetes.

Regular exercise makes a person feel alert, increases resistance to disease, and relieves feelings of depression and anxiety. Vigorous exercise also releases compounds called endorphins from the brain. Endorphins are compounds produced by the brain and their effects resemble the effects of morphine. Endorphins promote feelings of well-being.

Exercise creates its own nutrient demands within the body, including an increased need for water, calories, certain minerals, and some vitamins. The most crucial need is for fluids.

The evaporation of perspiration from the surface of the skin is the body's primary method of releasing the excess heat that accumulates in the muscles and internal organs during vigorous exercise. Adequate fluid must be present for this mechanism to function. In addition, loss of body water through perspiration can reduce the volume of blood. Reduction in blood results in thicker, more concentrated blood that is less able to penetrate muscle tissues and provide them with oxygen, fuel, and nutrients.

One of the first symptoms of dehydration is fatigue, as the muscles suffer from lack of oxygen and nutrients and from the accumulation of waste products in the cells. A rule of thumb is to replace 14 to 16 ounces of water for every pound of body weight lost during exercise. For individuals involved in a moderately vigorous fitness program, drink fluids before exercising, at 15 to 20 minute intervals during exercise, and after exercising. An intake of 6 to 8 glasses of fluids is recommended for sedentary adults who obtain little exercise. The best fluid to drink before and during exercise is water. Soft drinks and fruit juices are concentrated in sugars and cannot be absorbed quickly. If consumed, they should be diluted with at least two times their volume in water.[90]

Sodium needs do not increase with exercise, except for vigorously exercising athletes. Increasing sodium intake can do more harm than good, because it leads to dehydration.

Small amounts of potassium and magnesium are lost in perspiration.[91,92] Urinary excretion of magnesium also increases. Eating a balanced meal within a few hours after a vigorous workout is considered adequate to replace minerals that are lost. Potassium-rich foods include oranges, tomatoes, bananas, dried fruits, and nuts. Magnesium is found in nuts, meat, fish, dried beans and peas, dark green leafy vegetables, whole grains, and milk.

Excretion of chromium and zinc increases following exercise. Both minerals are required for the metabolism of sugar, which is a primary source of energy during exercise.[22] Good dietary sources of these minerals include whole grain breads and cereals, lean meat, and vegetables.

Some research indicates that extra vitamin E can prevent destruction of body cells from oxidation, a

24

process that increases during physical exertion.[93] Vitamin E is an antioxidant that protects cell membranes from the destructive substances such as free radicals. If the cell membrane is broken, harmful substances such as carcinogens (cancer-initiating substances) can enter the cell. Endurance exercise might increase the need for vitamin E to protect heart tissue and muscle from this damage.[94,95]

For the physically active person, adequate levels of carbohydrates are important. Carbohydrates increase energy levels and performance because they allow the body to store greater reserves of glycogen, a storage form of sugar used during exercise.[96] Pasta, potatoes, breads, rice, and cereals are excellent sources of complex carbohydrates. Whole grains contribute more trace nutrients and fiber than their refined counterparts such as white flour, white rice, and white bread.

Anytime energy needs in the body are increased, an extra need is created for the vitamins that metabolize protein, fat, and carbohydrates. Physically active adults need larger amounts of the vitamins thiamin, riboflavin, and niacin.[97] Good sources of these vitamins are whole grain breads and cereals.

Anemia might concern individuals who run or walk on a regular basis as a form of exercise. Excessive perspiration from all forms of exercise might increase iron losses through the skin.

Good sources of iron include red meat and dark poultry meat, dark green leafy vegetables, dry beans and peas, whole grains, peanut butter, potatoes, dried fruit, berries, and nuts. In addition, an excellent way to increase iron intake is to eat vitamin C-rich foods with iron-rich foods. Vitamin C interacts with iron to increase its absorption by as much as 50%.[98] Since individuals normally absorb only 2% to 10% of the iron in food, the combination of vitamin C and iron might be beneficial. Foods high in vitamin C include citrus fruits, tomatoes, cabbage, potatoes, dark green leafy vegetables such as broccoli, spinach, and chard, strawberries, green peppers, kiwi fruit, and cantaloupe.

Other nutrients important in the formation and maintenance of healthy red blood cells include vitamin B_6, folic acid, vitamin B_{12}, other B vitamins, vitamin E, copper, and protein.[99]

4
Acute Disease, Stress, and Nutrition

Nutritional needs increase during times of acute physiological stress, such as traumatic injury or burns, surgery, illness, and infection.[100] Stress hormones are secreted and cause numerous changes in nutrient metabolism and nutrient needs. The use and excretion of nutrients increase, energy needs increase, and gastrointestinal function and normal biochemical pathways are interrupted.[100] In addition, eating well while under stress is difficult.

Nutritional support is a major part of the therapeutic treatment for extensive burns. Nutritional care is crucial because nutrient losses are large as a result of loss of body tissues and the ensuing stress response and because there is extensive need for tissue to heal and new tissue to grow.[101] These processes depend on the available supply of nutrients.

Traumatic injury and second and third degree burns cause loss of fluids through burn sores, bleeding, or internal injuries. It is essential that these fluids be replaced.[101] Sodium, potassium, and chloride lost along with the fluids also must be replaced.

A greater calorie intake is required during times of stress, fever, and the healing of tissues. Starch from whole grain breads and cereals, vegetables, and dried beans and peas is the best dietary source of calories. These foods supply the B vitamins and trace minerals necessary to extract and use the contained calories and starch is easy to digest. Calorie needs might increase to 3,000 calories a day, and up to 8,000 calories a day.[100,101]

Vitamin C levels decrease in the the body during stress.[72,100] Vitamin C aids in tissue repair and wound healing and helps maintain healthy blood vessels. This vitamin might be given in doses of 100 to 300 mg up to 1 to 2 grams to patients who have burns. The Recommended Daily Allowance, or RDA, for healthy adults is 60 mg.[102] Although vitamin C does not prevent colds, it might reduce the symptoms and severity of a cold.[73-75] Vitamin C is found in citrus fruits, such as oranges, grapefruit, and tangerines, and most vegetables. Several servings of fruits and vegetables should be included in the diet each day.

The need for zinc increases during stress because zinc is excreted in in the urine.[1,103,104] Zinc aids in wound healing and helps maintain a healthy immune system. One symptom of zinc deficiency is altered taste, which can lead to loss of appetite. Copper also is excreted in the urine when an individual is suffering from stress. *(Table 4a)*

Magnesium, calcium, and vitamin A are excreted in the urine of trauma patients and might require replacement.[1,105-107] Calcium is lost from bones in varying amounts depending on hormonal state during stress.[108] Blood levels of vitamin A and iron are also low during stress.[1,109,110] Vitamin A protects a person from infections through its maintenance of healthy eyes, skin, mouth, lungs and other tissues.

Table 4a	The Zinc and Copper Content of Selected Foods		
Food	Serving Size	Zinc Content mg/serving	Copper Content mg/serving
Oysters, fresh	6 medium	124.9	14.2
Liver, beef	3 oz.	3.7	2.38
Bran flakes, 40%	1 c.	1.3	0.51
Swiss cheese	1 oz.	1.11	0.03
Milk, whole	1 c.	0.93	0.09
Egg	1 large	0.72	0.05
Potato, baked	1 medium	0.44	0.36
Spinach, cooked	1/2 c.	0.17	0.13
Banana	1 medium	0.04	0.26

If blood loss has been excessive because of injury or from repeated blood samples, anemia might develop and decrease the supply of oxygen to injured tissues. This necessitates formation of new red blood cells, a process that requires adequate iron, copper, vitamin C, folic acid, vitamins B_{12} and B_6, protein, and calories.[111-113]

Hospitalization and Surgery

The nutritional requirements for a surgical patient, while similar to those of a patient with a severe wound, infection, or injury, are complicated by the stress of illness that may precede hospitalization and by the stress of the hospital stay. Surveys indicate that up to 50% of patients in many hospitals suffer from malnutrition.[114] The surgical patient must be in an optimally nourished state prior to and after surgery to ensure a speedy recovery.[115] A healthy immune system depends on a high dietary intake of protein, calories, zinc, iron, selenium, vitamin C, vitamin E, vitamin A, vitamin B_6, and folic acid.[35,59] Malnutrition depresses immunity, delays wound healing, and increases susceptibility to infection.[33,59] Malnutrition delays recovery.[75,116]

A patient might enter the hospital in a nutritionally depleted state because of poor eating habits or poor nutrient absorption prior to illness. Frequent blood samples can leave a patient anemic and reduce the supply of oxygen to healing tissue. Fasting prior to diagnostic tests, X-rays, and surgery might further deplete nutrient stores.[114,117] The stress of hospitalization can cause a weight loss in the patient.[114,117] Malnutrition and weight loss can develop with progressive weakness, depression, apathy, irritability, and lethargy. Surgical wounds heal more slowly and infections are more likely to develop.[116]

During times of acute stress a diet of whole grain breads and cereals, vegetables and fruits, nuts and dried beans and peas, lean meats, chicken, fish, and low-fat dairy foods should be consumed. The goal of the diet is to provide the maximum amount of vitamins, minerals, fiber, and protein for the calories allotted. Foods that supply calories but little or no nutrients, such as fats and fatty foods, sugars, and highly processed foods, should be avoided or used with discretion.

5
Chronic Disease, Stress, and Nutrition

Numerous diseases are related to stress. These include cardiovascular disease and coronary heart disease, some forms of cancer, hypertension (high blood pressure), migraine headaches, ulcers, allergies, asthma, and depression.[118] Nutrition can affect these diseases.

Cardiovascular Disease, Stress, and Nutrition

Diseases of the heart and blood vessels are a major cause of death and disability in the United States.[119,120]

A particular personality pattern, called Type A personality, correlates with the development of cardiovascular disease (CVD). Type A people are competitive, high achievers, hostile and aggressive, have a sense of time urgency, and deny fatigue. People with Type A personalities are twice as likely to develop CVD than those with the more relaxed Type B personality.[121] *(Tables 5 and 6)*

The psychological stress caused by stressful life events, such as job dissatisfaction, money worries, and excessive work, are related to increased risk for heart disease.[121]

Table 5	Characteristics of Type A and Type B Personalities	
Personality Type Characteristics	**Type A**	**Type B**
Time sense	"Hurry Sickness": time-conscious, punctual, sense of urgency, impatience	Not concerned with time and deadlines
Timeframe	Short-term	Longer view
Speech	Fast, emphatic, interrupting	Slow
Attitude toward the future	Worrisome	Relaxed
Personality	Driving, aggressive	Relaxed
Typical work	Sales	Decision-making position
Natural work pace	Hurried	Slow
Reaction to stress symptoms	Ignore	Recognize and reduce
Temper	Easily angered	Slow to anger
Career pattern	Early success	Steady sustained success
Work/play style	Single sports, anxious to lead, competition	Team player, relaxation
Habits	Smoke, drink, overeat, drive fast, sleep poorly, over exercise	Moderation, moderate exercise, rest, relaxation
Social	Anxious for advancement and recognition	Casual
Patience	Little	Average

Table 6   Type A Behavior Revised

- If you are usually too busy, leave details to someone else whenever possible (the income tax return, fixing your car, office details).

- Move through your day slowly enough to experience beauty in your environment — on your way to school or work, for example.

- Learn to live with unfinished tasks.

- Leave enough time between activities so that you minimize overlap.

- Schedule only as many tasks each day as you can reasonably finish without pressure. Ask yourself what you can delegate.

- Leave time in your schedule for the unexpected.

- Leave early enough so that you need not rush to get where you are going, even if this means rising 20 minutes earlier in the morning.

- Say no to new opportunities or responsibilities if they would overload or rush your day.

- Take steps to "center," in order to know your priorities.

- Find a work environment that is not chronically high-pressured or harried. Avoid Type A organizations. Find another job if necessary.

- Avoid doing more than one thing at a time.

- Tell yourself at least once a day that failure seldom results from doing a job too slowly or too well. But failure often is caused by mistakes of judgment or from too much hurrying.

- Ask yourself at least once a week; apart from eternal distress and hurry, what is really important to me?

- Measure success by quality, rather than quantity.

(Continued on next page)

Table 6   Continued

- "Screen out" whenever possible, even if this risks disapproval or missing something you may have thought important. Then fully enjoy what you do choose.

- Surround yourself with symbols of tranquility: soft music, plants, pleasant colors, and lighting.

- Use your noon hour for deep relaxation, exercise, or something else which will slow you down, lift your spirits, and restore energy.

- Find time and space to be alone each day other than at your desk or in your car.

The stress hormones are apparently significant in the risk for developing cardiovascular disease. These hormones might accelerate the risk for cardiovascular disease because they increase blood pressure. Increased pressure in the arteries damages artery walls and encourages the formation of fat deposits.[121,122] Stress hormones also cause an increase in blood fats, including cholesterol. Cholesterol is a major contributor to atherosclerosis, which is hardening of the arteries.[123] The hormones also increase clumping of platelets, which are substances in the blood involved in clotting.[124,125] Arteries become clogged and narrowed, blood flow is blocked, and heart attack can occur. Biofeedback, meditation, and other techniques decrease adrenalin and help a person cope with stress.[126,120]

Reducing the intake of saturated fats and cholesterol is the primary way to prevent or treat CVD. Saturated fats in the diet are found primarily in foods from animal sources. Exceptions to this rule are palm and coconut oils, which are highly saturated. In addition, margarines and other hydrogenated vegetable fats contain saturated fats. Cholesterol is found only in foods from animal sources. Reductions in dietary cholesterol decrease cholesterol levels.[127,129] Because both saturated fat and cholesterol generally occur in the same foods, a reduction in one will usually mean a reduction in the other. *(Table 7, page 36)*

Some vitamins and minerals affect cholesterol levels in the blood. Deficiencies of flouride, copper, and chromium raise cholesterol[22,130,131] and an increased intake of these minerals might reduce blood cholesterol and lower the risk for developing CVD.[22,130] A magnesium deficiency is associated with arrhythmia (irregular heart beat) and supplementation might reduce a person's risk for developing cardiovascular disease.[132-134] Magnesium is lost from cells during stress, particularly in Type A individuals.[135,136]

Vitamin E reduces the symptoms of poor circulation in the legs caused by atherosclerosis.[137] A vitamin C deficiency also might be linked to an increased risk for developing cardiovascular disease.[138,139]

Coffee consumption might increase a person's risk for CVD. People who drink more than five cups of coffee a day have a higher risk of heart attack than people who do not drink coffee. Caffeine can produce irregular heart beats, especially in those with heart problems.[8]

The type of fiber called pectin, which is found primarily in apples and other fruits, lowers cholesterol levels by binding cholesterol in the small intestines and causing its excretion.[140] A diet high in foods

Table 7	Reducing The Fat In A Meal		
A Common High Fat Meal	**Grams of Fat**	**Skimmed Down Meal**	**Grams of Fat**
6 Oz. Sirloin Steak	20	6 Oz. Broiled Fish With Lemon	11
Tossed Salad With French Dressing	6	Tossed Salad With Vinegar	—
Green Beans With 1 Pat Margarine	4	Green Beans With Lemon, Basil or Marjoram	—
Baked Potato With 2 Pats Margarine	8	Baked Potato With 1 Pat Margarine	4
Roll With 1 Pat Margarine	6	Roll With 1/2 Pat Margarine	4
1 Cup Whole Milk	8	1 Cup Skim Milk	—
Apple Pie A La Mode	25	Cantaloupe	—
Coffee With Cream	2	Coffee, Black	—
Total	**79**	**Total**	**19**
79 × 9 = 711 Kcal		19 × 9 = 171 Kcal	
		These Simple Changes Reduce the Meal's Fat Content by 75%, and the Calories by 540.	

from animal sources and low in plant protein raises blood cholesterol.[141,142] Elevated blood cholesterol and CVD also might be prevented or treated by exercise, moderate alcohol consumption, the inclusion of fish in the diet, not smoking, and maintaining ideal weight.[120,143] *(Figure 3)*

Figure 3: Dietary Sources of Different Fibers

Fiber

Cellulose

Bran, whole grains, fruits, vegetables

Hemi-Cellulose

Bran, whole grains, fruits, vegetables

Lignin

Whole grains, vegetables (especially cabbage, broccoli, apples, strawberries)

Pectin

Apples, citrus fruits, nuts

Gums and Mucilages

Fruits, vegetables, grains

Cancer, Stress, and Nutrition

Psychological stress is associated with some types of cancer.[144] Loss, grief, hopelessness, and depression often precede cancer. Evidence suggests that a relationship exists between psychological stress and some forms of cancer including breast cancer, cervical cancer, leukemia, and lymphoma.

Cancer is the unrestrained growth of cells. Any cell can become a cancer cell if exposed to a carcinogen, which is a cancer-causing substance. Several dietary factors might be involved in cancer prevention such as fiber, vitamins A and E, and selenium.[145] In contrast, other dietary factors such as caffeine, fat, some food additives, and natural toxins are linked to an increased risk for cancer.[146,147]

Excessive fat intake, whether saturated or unsaturated, might contribute to cancer.[148] Fats in margarine and shortening also can increase the risk of cancer, as they leave the cell vulnerable to carcinogens.[148] A diet high in vegetable oils such as salad dressing, safflower and corn oils, or nuts and seeds, is linked to an increased incidence of some cancers.[149] A high fat intake also increases the risk for colon cancer.[148,150]

To reduce the risk of cancer, especially during times of stress, choose low-fat meats, chicken, fish, and low-fat dairy foods; bake, steam and broil rather than fry or saute; avoid sauces and gravies; and consume whole grain breads and cereals, dried beans and peas, and fresh fruits and vegetables.

Adequate fiber intake might help to partially counteract the effects of dietary fat, because certain types of fiber bind to fats in the intestines and carry them out of the body. Fiber also might dilute and speed up the passage of cancer-causing substances through the intestines.[151,152] *(Table 8)*

A diet high in vitamin A or its relative beta carotene might reduce the risk of some forms of cancers, including skin, lung, breast, and bladder cancer.[153-155] Vitamin A-deficient diets are associated with an increased risk for developing cancer.[156,157] Several servings daily of dark green or orange vegetables and fruits will provide the daily requirement for vitamin A and might help prevent cancer. *(Table 9, page 40)*

Table 8	A 45 Gram Fiber Menu		
	Meal	**Amount**	**Fiber**
Breakfast:	All Bran	1/3 cup	7.9
	Banana	1 medium	1.3
	Milk, 1%	1 cup	—
	Orange Juice	6 oz.	0.6
	Whole Wheat Bread	2 slices	5.4
	Jelly	1 tsp	—
		Total fiber content:	**15.2g**
Lunch:	Salad: Spinach	1 cup	2.2
	Carrots	1/4 cup	0.8
	Lima Beans	1/4 cup	1.8
	Tomato	1/4	0.5
	Cheese	2 oz.	—
	Dressing	1 to 1½ tbls	—
	Whole Wheat Roll	1	5.4
	Orange	1	3.8
		Total fiber content:	**14.5g**
Snack:	Tangerine	1	1.8
	Rye Crackers	2	1.5
		Total fiber content:	**3.3g**
Dinner:	Salmon	4 oz	—
	Baked potato, with skin	1 medium	5.2
	Yogurt dressing	2 tbls	—
	Broccoli	2/3 cup	3.2
	Dinner salad	1 to 1½ cups	2.0
	Dressing	2 tsp	—
		Total fiber content:	**10.4g**
Snack:	Graham crackers	2	1.3
		Total fiber content:	**1.3g**
		Menu Total fiber content:	**44.7g**

Table 9:	Beta Carotene (Vitamin A)	
Food	**Seving**	**Vitamin A (as Carotene) (micrograms)**
Collard greens	1 cup cooked	8,892 mcg
Spinach	1 cup raw	2,676
Squash:		
acorn	1 cup	1,722
Cantaloupe	1/2	5,544
Broccoli	1 cup cooked	2,320
Peaches	1 large	1,218

Some vitamins and minerals act as antioxidants to prevent cells from damage and possibly cancer. Low amounts of selenium in the diet are associated with an increased risk for cancer.[79-81] There is a possibility of a selenium deficiency in the American diet since the selenium content of food is only as good as the selenium content of the soil in which the food is grown. Many areas of the country, including parts of the midwest, pacific northwest, and New England, have soil that is low in selenium.[82] Vitamins E, C, and A function with selenium as antioxidants and aid in the protection of the body's cells.[158] In addition, vitamin C inhibits the activity of some cancer-causing substances called nitrites in processed meats and helps prevent stomach cancer.[159]

A family of vegetables, called the cruciferous vegetables, might reduce the risk of cancer.[160] The protective effect of these vegetables is not a result of their vitamin A or vitamin C content, but rather is attributed to other, non-nutritive substances called indoles. The cruciferous vegetables are cabbage, cauliflower, broccoli, Brussels sprouts, and kohlrabi.

In addition, alcohol, and salt-cured, smoked, and nitrite-cured foods increase the risk for cancer by producing cancer-causing substances.[161] Obesity can increase the risk of developing some cancers. Weight loss in the obese might be a way to reduce this risk.[162]

Although there are numerous cancer-promoting substances it is thought that nature provides a balance by including cancer-inhibiting substances at the same time.[147] Adequate levels of all nutrients might provide the state of health required to respond to these potential stressors. A healthy immune system is also an important part of the defense against cancer-causing substances.

Hypertension, Stress, and Diet

An elevation in blood pressure is one of the responses of the body to stress. This is part of the "fight or flight" response. Under continued stress, however, blood pressure can remain high and result in hypertension. A high sodium (salt) diet is associated with hypertension.[163-165] *(Table 10, page 42)* Low magnesium and calcium levels also might be a risk factor for hypertension.[166-168] Deficiencies of other nutrients have been associated with hypertension, including potassium, vitamin A, and vitamin C.[167]

Depression, Sleeping Problems, and Nutrition

Chemicals in the brain affect both mood and behavior. Serotonin is one of many chemicals necessary for

Table 10	Where's The Sodium?
	The Salt Shaker
	Processed Foods
	Canned Soups, Meats, Chili
	Baking Mixes
	Pickles, Seasoning Mixtures
	Catsup, Steak Sauce, Soy Sauce, Etc.
	Frozen Entrees/Dinners
	Side Dishes (Macaroni and Cheese, Seasoned Noodles, Etc.)
	Canned Vegetables
	Frozen Vegetables
	Baking Powder and Soda
	Luncheon Meats
	Cured Meats
	Hard Cheeses
	Monosodium Glutamate and Other Food Additives
	Fast Food — Hamburgers, Shakes, Fries, Pizza, Chicken, Salad Bar

normal nerve transmission. Depression, wakefulness, and a lowered tolerance to pain might result without enough of this chemical.[169] A high-carbohydrate meal, combined with tryptophan supplements, can increase serotonin levels in the brain. A high protein meal lowers serotonin.[169,170]

The depression sometimes experienced by dieters might be caused by eating too many high protein foods and too few starches, which reduces serotonin levels.[171] Both tryptophan and vitamin B_6 are needed by the brain to make serotonin and supplements of vitamin B_6 might help treat depression.[172]

Tryptophan might be useful in the treatment of some stress-related sleep disorders.[173] Because this amino acid affects the production of chemicals involved in nerve transmission and thought and personality processes, long-term supplementation should be supervised by a physician.

Headaches, Stress, and Nutrition

Migraine headaches that are stress-related might be triggered by food allergies. Usually the intestinal tract responds to an allergy-producing food, but in migraine headaches the brain reacts. Foods that might trigger migraines include cheese and milk, chocolate, red wine, coconut, wheat, cola drinks, coffee and tea, pork and beef, grapes and citrus fruits, corn, cane sugar, dried beans and peas, and yeast.[174] Some non-migraine headaches are caused by additives in foods such as monosodium glutamate, a flavor enhancer used in Chinese cooking.[174,175]

To determine if headaches are caused by food intolerances, eliminate all suspected foods from the diet. After two weeks, add one food at a time to the diet and observe any adverse reactions. The foods should be added slowly to avoid confusion over which food produced the effects. This process should be done under the supervision of a physician.

Lack of Exercise, Stress, and Nutrition

Leading a sedentary life creates its own form of nutritional stress. For bones to maintain density and strength throughout adulthood, new supplies of calcium, phosphorus, and magnesium must be deposited in them daily. Even if adequate amounts of these nutrients are consumed, unless an individual exercises, the bones are less efficient in pulling these nutrients from the blood. The pressure on bones produced by physical activity is the necessary ingredient. Lack of exercise and poor calcium intake can contribute to osteoporosis, a condition that causes porous, brittle bones that are prone to breaks and fractures.[176] A diet that is high in calcium, combined with physical activity, can help prevent this bone loss in later life.

Muscles require a stimulus to absorb nutrients from the blood. Unless muscles are used and exercised regularly, the muscles break down and shrink in size, which might lead to decreased strength and poor muscle tone.[177]

With fat intake high in the average diet, imbalances of blood fats are common. Exercise decreases harmful blood fats and increases the proportion of beneficial blood fats.[178] In addition, exercise increases fitness of the heart and lungs.[179]

6
Guidelines for Coping with Stress

Preparing for Stress with Nutrition

The best defense for the demands of stress is a healthy body with tissues that contain optimal amounts of nutrients.[108]

Include two or more servings of vitamin C-rich foods such as citrus fruits, dark green leafy vegetables, broccoli, or cabbage in the daily diet. Food high in vitamin A (dark green or orange vegetables) and in folic acid (dark green vegetables and orange juice) should also be included in the diet each day. Avoid exposing produce that has been cut or trimmed to air and light, and consume this produce within a day or two to minimize nutrient losses. Combine vitamin C-rich foods with iron-rich foods at the same meals to maximize iron absorption.

The best way to achieve a high nutrient intake is to choose whole, unprocessed foods such as whole grain breads and cereals, dried beans and peas, fresh fruits and vegetables, lean meats, and nonfat or low-fat milk. Whole wheat breads and cereals, brown rice, and other whole grains provide folic acid, fiber, vitamin B_6, vitamin E, magnesium, chromium, and zinc.

Sources of iron are lean meats, dried beans and peas, and dark green leafy vegetables. Zinc and magnesium can be obtained from foods such as lean meats, seafood, dried beans and peas, and whole grain breads and cereals. Chromium is supplied by whole grain breads and cereals and lean meats. Foods rich in vitamin B_6 include lean meat, chicken, fish, and dried beans and peas. Potassium is obtained from fresh fruits and vegetables consumed in the diet each day.

Cutting back on foods high in sugar, fat, caffeine, and sodium can reduce the risk of developing heart disease, cancer, hypertension, and other stress-related diseases. Convenience foods are often high in sugar, fat, and sodium, and should be kept to a minimum.

Consume fish, poultry, lean meat, skim milk cheeses and legumes as protein sources rather than fatty meats and cheeses. Luncheon meats and bacon are high in fat and sodium, and might increase the risk for developing cancer because of the sodium nitrates and nitrites used to cure and color the product.[159] Nonfat and low-fat milk and milk products provide valuable calcium and other nutrients without the fat found in their whole milk counterparts.

Drink plenty of water to provide the cells with ample fluid and to aid the kidneys in flushing out waste products.

Preparing For Stress with Exercise

Exercise is an important component of stress prevention. Exercise maintains healthy bones, muscles, heart, and lungs. Exercise also provides the emotional and mental relief that helps a person cope with and prevent stress.

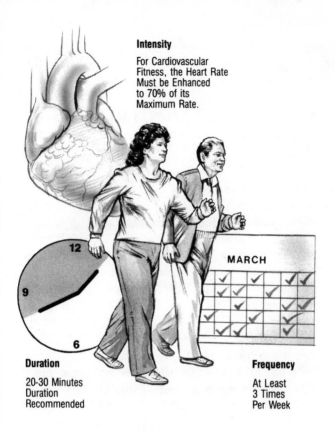

Intensity

For Cardiovascular
Fitness, the Heart Rate
Must be Enhanced
to 70% of its
Maximum Rate.

MARCH

Duration

20-30 Minutes
Duration
Recommended

Frequency

At Least
3 Times
Per Week

Figure 4. The 3 keys to exercise.

Three sessions a week of aerobic exercise lasting 20
to 30 minutes are a minimum to provide improvement
in cardiovascular fitness. *(Figure 4)* Walking, jogging,
and jumping rope are examples of aerobic exercise
and all place beneficial pressure on bones, heart, and
lungs. These exercises also increase muscle tone.
Stretching and warm-up exercises prior to physical

activity and cool down exercises afterwards are important components of a well-rounded fitness program.

Nutrition During Times of Stress

The three energy fuels, protein, fat, and carbohydrate, are used in increased quantities during times of severe stress. If the stress is so severe that an individual is not eating, fuel must come from internal sources, such as muscles, fat stores, and other tissues. Stores of carbohydrate will be used up in a day or two, and breakdown of muscle will occur. Carbohydrate foods are particularly important because the calories they provide prevent dietary protein from being used for energy. Instead, protein can be used to maintain a healthy immune system and adequate muscle size, to regulate the normal acidity of the blood, and to synthesize the millions of substances needed to regulate body processes.

Avoid salty foods to help prevent elevated blood pressure. Examples of salty foods are commercial snack foods, canned and dried soups, luncheon meats, convenience foods, and pickled foods. Consume an adequate intake of B complex vitamins and vitamin C, along with plenty of calcium, magnesium, zinc, iron, vitamin A, and vitamin E. If dietary intake is below 1,500 calories, a multiple vitamin/mineral supplement might be needed.[180] Consume adequate fluids, but consume caffeine-containing beverages and alcohol in moderation. Limit sugar intake to minimal amounts.

Eat foods rich in vitamin C (citrus fruits, berries, broccoli, tomatotes), every day, as well as foods high in potassium (tomatoes, bananas, dark green leafy vegetables, dates, citrus fruits). Low-fat milk, yogurt, and cheese might help prevent loss of calcium from bones.

Eat regular meals. Include two or more servings of complex carbohydrate foods, fruits, and vegetables at each meal with a smaller amount of a protein-rich food. Stressful times are not the time to diet. Dieting will add to the metabolic stress of the body and might cause depression. Take the time to slow down and relax at mealtimes to facilitate absorption of nutrients. If an individual is preparing meals for someone under stress, make a special effort to make the table look nice and the food tasty, colorful, and appetizing.

Exercise should be included in the daily routine even when a person is not in the mood for physical activity. A short, brisk walk can release tension and elevate mood. If stress is so severe that appetite is suppressed, eating may cause nausea and vomiting and a person should wait until he or she is calmer.

A day should not go by without making an effort to eat. It may be easier to eat small meals and snacks throughout the day rather than trying to eat a large meal.

Recovering From Stress

Body stores of nutrients need to be replenished, particularly carbohydrate, protein, calcium, potassium, vitamin C, B complex vitamins, iron, zinc, and magnesium, when recovering from stress. Adequate calories need to be consumed. More calories should be consumed if weight has been lost. If possible, use physical activity to help restore nutrients to tissues. Even short walks are beneficial. If weight was gained through overeating, gradually work the diet back to a normal pattern.

How Stressful Is Your Diet?

Use the following checklist of healthy, anti-stress food choices and eating patterns to see how your diet measures up.

- Relaxed, pleasant mealtimes.
- Breakfast eaten daily.
- Two to three servings of low fat protein foods daily (fish, poultry, lean meat, dried beans and peas).
- Half the protein servings come from animal sources and half from plant foods to avoid excess fat (refried beans with a tortilla, split pea soup with a whole grain muffin, etc.).
- High fat meats are seldom consumed (bacon, sausage, luncheon meat, fried chicken or fish, steak and other fatty beef cuts, corned beef, ham, etc.).
- A minimum of six servings of breads, cereal, pasta, or grain daily, more if calorie needs permit.
- At least 50% of bread, grains, and cereal servings are whole grain versions.
- Two to four servings of nonfat or low-fat milk products daily (milk, yogurt, buttermilk, low-fat cheeses and low-fat cottage cheese) or equivalent calcium from dark green leafy vegetables, ground sesame seeds, and other non-dairy sources, and/or calcium supplements.
- At least four servings of fruits and vegetables daily.

- Majority of fruit and vegetable servings are fresh or frozen rather than canned.
- One vegetable serving is high in folic acid, such as spinach, chard, broccoli, romaine or other leaf lettuce, peas, or green beans.
- One or two fruit or vegetable servings are high in vitamin C, such as orange juice, grapefruit juice, broccoli, and other fruits and vegetables.
- One fruit or vegetable serving is high in beta-carotene (the plant form of vitamin A), such as dark green and orange vegetables (yams, carrots, spinach, broccoli, asparagus).
- Iron foods (meats, legumes, grains, vegetables) are consumed with vitamin C foods to assist iron absorption.
- One tablespoon of a polyunsaturated vegetable oil daily (used in salad dressing, cooking, etc.) or 1/4 cup nuts or seeds.
- Total fat intake not more than 30% of total calories, and not less than 10% (1 teaspoon of fat = 5 grams = 45 calories).
- Intake of added fats is low: butter, margarine, gravy, cream, non-dairy creamer, shortenings, salad dressings, oil, etc.
- Intake of salt and sodium is low.
- Consumption of processed, convenience foods and fast foods is infrequent.
- Sugar intake is low (table sugar, honey, corn syrup, pancake syrup, etc.); no more than 10% of total calories (1 teaspoon sugar = 5 grams = 20 calories).
- Caffeine intake is low to moderate (no more than two cups a day).

- Fluid intake (caffeine-free and alcohol-free) is at least 6 to 8 glasses daily.
- Processed foods containing artificial colorings and flavorings, sodium nitrite and sodium nitrate, added salt, sodium-containing additives, sugar, and hydrogenated vegetable oils are limited to infrequent consumption.
- Adequate calories are consumed; if attempting weight loss, intake is not under 1,200 calories for women, 1,500 calories for men.
- Food is enjoyed; you are not overly anxious about caloric intake.

A healthful, anti-stress diet is one that contains whole, fresh, unprocessed foods. Eat plenty of unrefined complex carbohydrates, consume a wide variety of foods from all food groups, and enjoy your food. Doing this increases your intake of all nutrients and minimizes taking in too much of any one nutrient or toxin in a particular food.

References

1. Nutritional demands imposed by stress. *Dairy Council Digest* 1980; 51:31-35.
2. Greenberg J: *Comprehensive Stress Management.* Dubuque, Iowa, William C Brown Co., 1984, pp 11-38.
3. Ibid, pp 10-11.
4. Ibid, p 214.
5. Hamilton E, Whitney E: *Understanding Nutrition,* ed 3. St. Paul, Minn, West Publishing Co, 1984, pp 83-84, 113, 305-310, 382, 562.
6. Chenault A: *Nutrition and Health.* New York, Holt Rinehart and Winston, 1984, pp 118, 171, 248-254, 394-395.
7. Hamilton E, Whitney E: *Understanding Nutrition,* ed 3. St. Paul, Minn, West Publishing Co, 1984, pp 142,166.
8. Ibid, p 183.
9. Greenberg J: *Comprehensive Stress Management.* Dubuque, Iowa, William C Brown Co, 1984, p 214.
10. Hamilton E, Whitney E: *Understanding Nutrition,* ed 3. St. Paul, Minn, West Publishing Co, 1984, pp 83-84, 208-210, 305-310, 562.
11. Chenault A: *Nutrition and Health.* New York, Holt Rinehart and Winston, 1984, pp 118, 171, 499, 513.
12. Hamilton E, Whitney E: *Understanding Nutrition,* ed 3. St. Paul, Minn, West Publishing Co, 1984, pp 561-562.
13. Reed P: *Nutrition: An Applied Science,* St. Paul, Minn, West Publishing Co, 1980, p 461.
14. Williams S: *Nutrition and Diet Therapy,* ed 5. St. Louis, Missouri, Times Mirror/Mosby College Publishing, 1985, p 155.
15. Dawber T, Kannel W, Gordon T: Coffee and cardiovascular disease: Observations from the Framingham Study. *N Eng J Med* 1974; 291:871-74.
16. Institute of Food Technologist's Expert Panel on Food Safety and Nutrition: Caffeine. *Contempory Nutrition* 1984; 9:1-2.
17. Snowdon D, Phillips R: Coffee consumption and risk of fatal cancers. *Am J Pub Health* 1984; 74:820.

18. Pozniak P: The carcinogenicity of caffeine and coffee: A review. *J Am Diet Assoc.* 1985; 85:1127-1133.

19. *Dietary Goals for the United States.* US Senate Select Committee on Nutrition and Human Needs. Washington DC, US Government Printing Office, 1977, pp 43-47.

20. Hamilton E, Whitney E: *Understanding Nutrition,* ed 3. St. Paul, Minn, West Publishing Co, 1984, p 278.

21. Briggs G, Calloway D: *Nutrition and Physical Fitness,* 11 ed. New York, Holt, Rinehart and Winston, 1984, p 240.

22. Langseth L, Dowd J: Glucose tolerance and hyperkinesis. *Food Cosmet Toxicol* 1978; 16:129.

23. Mertz W: Chromium: An essential nutrient. *Contemporary Nutrition* 1982; 7:1-2.

24. Siminoff M: Chromium deficiency and cardiovascular risk: A review. *Cardio Res* 1984; 18:591-596.

25. Anderson R, Kozlovsky A: Chromium intake, absorption and excretion of subjects consuming self-selected diets. *Am J Clin Nutr* 1985; 41:1177-1183.

26. Hamilton E, Whitney E: *Understanding Nutrition,* ed 3. St. Paul, Minn, West Publishing Co, 1984, p 435.

27. Boyle E, Mondscheim B, Dash H: Chromium depletion in the pathogenesis of diabetes and atherosclerosis. *S Med J* 1977; 70:1449-1453.

28. Dietary Goals for the United States. US Senate Select Committee on Nutrition and Human Needs. Washington DC, US Government Printing Office, 1977.

29. Apfelbaum M: Adaptation to changes in caloric intake. *Progress in Food and Nutritional Science* 1978; 2:543-559.

30. Madden C: What keeps obese persons obese? *Can Assoc Health, Phys Ed, Rec J* 1983; Jul-Aug:5-7.

31. Wooley S, Wooley O: Obesity in women: A closer look at the facts. *Women's Studies Internat Quarterly* 1979; 2:69-79.

32. Chenault A: *Nutrition and Health.* New York, Holt Rinehart and Winston, 1984, p 497.

33. Chandra R, Tejpar S: Diet and immunocompetence. *Int J Imm* 1983; 5:175-180.

34. Chenault A: *Nutrition and Health.* New York, Holt Rinehart and Winston, 1984, p 513.

35. *Dietary Goals for the United States.* US Senate Select Committee on Nutrition and Human Needs. Washington DC, US Government Printing Office, 1977, p XXXIV

36. Ernsberger E: Yo-yo hypertension: The death of dieting. *Am Health* 1985; 4: 29-33.

37. Garrison R, Somer E: *The Nutrition Desk Reference.* Keats Publishing Co, New Canaan, Conn. 1985, pp 220-221.

38. Hamilton E, Whitney E: *Understanding Nutrition,* ed 3. St. Paul, Minn, West Publishing Co, 1984, p 313.

39. Shaw S, Leiver C: *Nutrition and Alcoholism,* in Goodhart R, Shills M(eds), *Modern Nutrition in Health and Disease* ed 6. Philadelphia, Lea and Febiger, 1980, pp 1220-1240.

40. Lieber C: Alcohol-nutrition interaction. *Contemporary Nutrition* 1983; 8:1.

41. Hamilton E, Whitney E: *Understanding Nutrition,* ed 3. St. Paul, Minn, West Publishing Co, 1984, pp 306-308.

42. Shaw S, Leiver: *Nutrition and Alcoholism,* in Goodhart R, Shills M (eds), *Modern Nutrition in Health and Disease* ed 6. Philadelphia, Lea and Febiger, 1980, pp 1226-1227.

43. Hamilton E, Whitney E: *Understanding Nutrition,* ed 3. St. Paul, Minn, West Publishing Co, 1984, p 309.

44. Ibid, pp 25, 309, 416.

45. Garrison R, Somer E: *The Nutrition Desk Reference.* New Canaan, Conn, Keats Publishing Co, 1985, p 48.

46. *Recommended Dietary Allowances,* 9th ed. The National Research Council, National Academy of Sciences, Washington DC, 1980, p 97.

47. Garrison R, Somer E: *The Nutrition Desk Reference.* New Canaan, Conn, Keats Publishing Co, 1985, pp 49, 94-95.

48. Hamilton E, Whitney E: *Understanding Nutrition,* ed 3. St. Paul, Minn, West Publishing Co, 1984, pp 305-312.

49. Garrison R, Somer E: *The Nutrition Desk Reference.* New Canaan, Conn, Keats Publishing Co, 1985, p 135.

50. Watson R: Nutrition and Immunity. *Contemporary Nutrition* 1981; 6:1-2.

51. Schleifer S, Keller S, Stein M: Stress effects on immunity. *Psychiat J U Ottawa* 1985; 10:125-131.

52. Hill C, Greer W, Felsenfield O: Psychological stress, early response to foreign protein, and blood cortisol in vervets. *Psychosom Med* 1967; 29:279-283.

53. Petrovskii I: Problems of nervous control in immunity reactions: The influence of experimental neurosis on immunity reactions. *Ah Mikrobiol Epidermiol Immunobiol* 1961; 32:63-69.

54. Vessey S: Effects of grouping on levels of circulating antibodies in mice. *Proc Soc Biol* 1964; 115:252-255.

55. Gisler R: Stress and the hormonal regulation of the immune response in mice. *Psychother Psychosom* 1974; 23:197-208.

56. Monjan A, Collector M: Stress-induced modulation of the immune response. *Science* 1977; 196:307-308.

57. Helsing K, Scklo M, Comstock G: Factors associated with mortality after widowhood. *Am J Pub Health* 1981; 71:802-809.

58. Cappel R, Gregoire F, Thiry L, et al: Antibody and cell-mediated immunity to herpes simplex virus in psychotic depression. *J Clin Psychiatry* 1978; 39:266-268.

59. Kronfol Z, Silva J, Greden J, et al: Impaired lymphocyte function in depressive illness. *Life Sci* 1983; 33:241-247.

60. Dreizen S: Nutrition and the immune response. *Internat J Vit Res* 1973; 49:223-228.

61. Blaszek I, Math G: Nutrition and immunity (review). *Biomed Par* 1984; 38:187-193.

62. Fernandes G, Nair M, Onoe K, et al: Impairment of cell-mediated immunity functions by dietary zinc deficiency in mice. *Proc Nat Acad Sci* 1979; 76:457.

63. Sugarman B: Zinc and infection (review). *Rev Infec D* 1983; 5:137.

64. Fischer P, Giroux A, L'Abbe M: Effect of zinc supplementation on copper status in adult man. *Am J Clin N* 1984; 40:743-646.

65. Chandra R: Excessive intake of zinc impairs immune response. *JAMA* 1984; 252:1443-1446.

66. Czajka-Narins D, Haddy T, Kallen D: Nutrition and social correlates in iron deficiency anemia. *Am J Clin Nutr* 1978; 31:955-960.

67. Chandra R: Trace element regulation of immunity and infection. *J Am Col N* 1985; 4:5-16.

68. Hamilton E, Whitney E: *Understanding Nutrition,* ed 3. St. Paul, Minn, West Publishing Co, 1984, pp 324-326.

69. Nuwayri-Salti N, Murad T: Immunologic and anti-suppressant effects of vitamin A. *Pharmacol* 1985; 30:181-187.

70. Sidell N, Famatiga E, Golub S: Immunological aspects of retinoids in humans. II. Retinoic acid enhances induction of hemolytic plaqueforming cells. *Cell Immun* 1984; 88:374-381.

71. Pardue S, Thaxton J: Evidence for amelioration of steroid immunosuppression by ascorbic acid. *Poultry Sci* 1984; 63:1262-1268.

72. Kallner A: Influence of vitamin C Status on the urinary excretion of catecholamines in stress. *Human Nutr: Clin Nutr* 1983; 37:405.

73. Vitamin C and the common cold. Committee on Drugs, American Academy of Pediatrics. *Nutr Rev* 1974; Jul (supp):39-40.

74. Anderson T, Reid D, Beaton G: Vitamin C and the common cold: A double-blind trial. *Can Med Assoc J* 1972; 107:503-508.

75. Coulehan J: Ascorbic acid and the common cold. *Postgrad Med* 1979; 66:153-160.

76. McCord J: Oxygen-derived free radicals in post-ischemic tissue injury. *N Eng J Med* 1985; 312:159-163.

77. Hamilton E, Whitney E: *Understanding Nutrition,* ed 3. St. Paul, Minn, West Publishing Co, 1984, pp 295-296, 340, 435-436.

78. Packer L, Smith J: Extension of the lifespan of cultured normal human diploid cells by vitamin E. *Proc Nat Acad Sci* 1974; 71:4763-4767.

79. Griffin A: Role of selenium in the chemoprevention of cancer. *Adv Cancer Res* 1979; 29:419-442.

80. Willet W, Polk B, Morris J, et al: Prediagnostic serum selenium and risk of cancer. *Lancet* 1983; 2:130-134.

81. Spallholz J: Selenium: What role in immunity and immune cytotoxicity?, in Spallholz J, Martin J, Gan-

ther H (eds), *Selenium in Biology and Medicine.* Westport, Conn, AVI Publishing, 1981,pp 1033-1117.

82. Shamberger R, Tytkos S, Willis C: Antioxidants and Cancer. *Arch Environ Health* 1976; 31:231-235.

83. Garrison R, Somer E: *The Nutrition Desk Reference.* New Canaan, Conn, Keats Publishing Co, 1985, p 101.

84. Smith J: The impact of smoking on serum vitamin C levels. *Fed Proc* 1984; 43:861.

85. Garrison R, Somer E: *The Nutrition Desk Reference.* New Canaan, Conn, Keats Publishing Co, 1985, pp 53-54.

86. US Dept of Health and Welfare: *Healthy People, The Surgeon General's Report on Health Promotion and Disease Prevention.* Washington DC, US Government Printing Office, 1979, DHEW (PHS) Publication # 79-55071, p 57.

87. *Recommended Dietary Allowances,* ed 9. The National Research Council, National Academy of Sciences, Washington DC, 1980, p 74.

88. Nutritional Demands imposed by stress. *Dairy Council Digest* 1980; 51:31-35.

89. Goodhart R, Shills M (eds): *Modern Nutrition in Health and Disease,* ed 6. Philadelphia, Lea and Febiger, 1980, p 1050.

90. Fink W: Fluid intake for maximizing athletic performance, in *Nutrition and Athletic Performance,* Haskel W, Skala J, Whittam J (eds). Palo Alto, California, Bull Publishing Co, 1982, p 59.

91. Garrison R, Somer E: *The Nutrition Desk Reference.* New Canaan, Conn, Keats Publishing Co, 1985, p 73.

92. Goodhart R, Shills M (eds): *Modern Nutrition in Health and Disease,* ed 6. Philadelphia, Lea and Febiger, 1980, pp 310-311.

93. Garrison R, Somer E: The Nutrition Desk Reference. New Canaan, Conn, Keats Publishing Co, 1985, p 40.

94. Aikawa K: Exercise endurance training alters vitamin E tissue levels in red blood cell hemolosis in rodents. *Biosci Rep* 1984; 4:253-257.

95. Garrison R, Somer E: *The Nutrition Desk Reference.* New Canaan, Conn, Keats Publishing Co, 1985, pp 174-175.

96. Ibid, pp 13-14
97. *Recommended Dietary Allowances* ed 9. The National Research Council, Washington DC, National Academy of Sciences, 1980, pp 82-92.
98. Garrison R, Somer E: *The Nutrition Desk Reference.* New Canaan, Conn, Keats Publishing Co, 1985, p 67.
99. Ibid, pp 24-25, 40-41, 43-45, 47-48, 50-51, 63
100. Kipp D: Stress and nutrition. *Contemporary Nutrition* 1984; 9(7):1.
101. Gastineau C, Myers M, Sandstead H, et al: Nutrition in trauma and burns. *Dialogues in Nutrition* 1977; 2(1).
102. *Recommended Dietary Allowances,* ed 9. The National Research Council, National Academy of Sciences, Washington DC, 1980, pp 73-74
103. Prasad A: Nutritional zinc today. *Nutr Today* 1981; 16:4.
104. Prasad A: Clinical, biochemical and nutritional spectrum of zinc deficiency in human subjects: An update. *Nutr Rev* 1983; 41:197.
105. Classen H: Stress and Magnesium. *Artery* 1981; 9:182-189.
106. Beisel W, in McKigney J, Munro H (eds), *Nutrient Requirements in Adolescence.* Cambridge, Mass, MIT Press, 1976, pp 257-278.
107. Scrimshaw N: Effect of infection on Nutrient Requirements. *Am J Clin Nutr* 1977; 30:1536-1544.
108. Hamilton E, Whitney E: *Understanding Nutrition,* ed 3. St. Paul, Minn, West Publishing Co, 1984, p 187.
109. Rai K, Courtemanche A: Vitamin A assay in burned patients. *J Trauma* 1975; 5:419.
110. Hoffman J, Buckberg G: Pathophysiology of subendocardial ischaemia. *Br Med J* 1975; 1:76-79.
111. Pike R, Brown M: *Nutrition — An Integrated Approach,* ed 2. New York, John Wiley and Sons, Inc., 1975, pp 120, 197, 608.
112. Hamilton E, Whitney E: *Understanding Nutrition,* ed 3. St. Paul, Minn, West Publishing Co, 1984, pp 128, 274, 410, 415, 433
113. Briggs G, Calloway D: *Nutrition and Physical Fitness,* 11 ed. New York, Holt, Rinehart and Winston, 1984, pp 68, 270-271, 278, 283, 309, 394.

114. Blackburn G, Chernoff R, Howard L, Shils M: Malnutrition in the hospital. *Dialogues in Nutrition* 1977:2.

115. Hill G, Pickford I, Young G, et al: Malnutrition in surgical patients. An unrecognized problem. *Lancet* 1977; 1:689.

116. Butterworth C: The skeleton in the hospital closet. *Nutr Today* 1974; Mar-Apr:4-8.

117. Weinsier R, Hunker E, Krumdiek C, et al: Hospital malnutrition — a prospective evaluation of general medical patients during the course of hospitalization. *Am J Clin Nutr* 1979; 32:418-426.

118. Selye H: *The Stress of Life.* New York, McGraw-Hill Book Co, 1976.

119. Stamler J: Public health aspects of optimal serum lipid-lipoprotein levels. *Prev Med* 1979; 8:733.

120. Stamler J: Major coronary risk factors before and after myocardial infection. *Postgrad Med* 1975; 57:25.

121. Glass D: Stress, behavior patterns and coronary disease. *Am Sci* 1977; 65:177-188.

122. Ardlie N, Glew G, Schwartz C: Influence of catecholamines on nucleotide-induced platelet aggression. *Nature* 1966; 212:415-417.

123. Garrison R, Somer E: *The Nutrition Desk Reference.* New Canaan, Conn, Keats Publishing Co, 1985, pp 152-153.

124. Friedman M, Rosenman R: Association of specific overt behavior pattern with blood and cardiovascular findings. *JAMA* 1959; 169:1286-1296.

125. Friedman M, Rosenman R, Carroll V: Changes in the serum cholesterol and bloodclotting time in men subject to cyclic variation of ocupational stress. *Circulation* 1958; 17:852-861.

126. Garrison R, Somer E: *The Nutrition Desk Reference.* New Canaan, Conn, Keats Publishing Co, 1985, p 97.

127. Hamilton E, Whitney E: *Understanding Nutrition,* ed 3. St. Paul, Minn, West Publishing Co, 1984, pp 102, 117-118.

128. Chenault A: *Nutrition and Health.* New York, Holt Rinehart and Winston, 1984, pp 213-214.

129. Garrison R, Somer E: *The Nutrition Desk Reference.* New Canaan, Conn, Keats Publishing Co, 1985, pp 160-161.

130. Ibid, p 110.

131. Ibid, p 112.

132. Supplementation of human diets with vitamin E. Committee on Nutritional Misinformation, Food and Nutrition Board, National Research Council. *Nutr Rev* 1974; Jul (Suppl):37-38.

133. Turlataty P, Altura B: Magnesium deficiency produces spasms of coronary arteries: Relationship to etiology of sudden death ischemic heart disease. *Science* 1980; 208:198-200.

134. Cohen L: Magnesium sulphate and digitalistoxic arrhythmias. *JAMA* 1983; 209:2808.

135. Henrotte J, Plouin P, Levy-Leboyer C, et al: Blood and urinary magnesium, zinc, calcium, free fatty acids, and catecholamines in Type A and Type B subjects. *J Am Col Nutr* 1985; 4:165-172.

136. Karppanen H: Epidemiological studies on the relationship between magnesium intake and cardiovascular diseases. *Artery* 1981; 9:190.

137. Haeger A: A longterm study of alpha-tocopherol in intermittent claudication. *NY Acad Sci* 1982; 392:369-375.

138. Ginter E: Ascorbic acid in cholesterol and bile metabolism. *Ann NY Acad Sci* 1975; 258:410-421.

139. Bates C, Burr M, Leger A: Vitamin C, high density lipoproteins, and heart disease in elderly subjects. *Age and Aging* 1979; 8:177-182.

140. Anderson J, Chen W: Plant fiber, carbohydrate and lipid metablosism. *Am J Clin Nutr* 1979; 32:346-363.

141. Hamilton E, Whitney E: *Nutrition Concepts and Controversies.* St. Paul, Minn, West Publishing Co, 1982, p 138.

142. Phillips R: Coronary heart disease mortality among Seventh-Day Adventists with differing dietary habits: A preliminary report. *Am J Clin Nutr* 1978; 31:S191.

143. Hamilton E, Whitney E: *Understanding Nutrition,* ed 3. St. Paul, Minn, West Publishing Co, 1984, p 120.

144. Hurst M, Jenkins C, Rose R: The relation of psychological stress to onset of medical illness. *Annual Rev Med* 1976; 27:173-176.
145. Hamilton E, Whitney E: *Understanding Nutrition,* ed 3. St. Paul, Minn, West Publishing Co, 1984, pp 71, 331, 436.
146. Hausman P: *Foods That Fight Cancer.* New York, Rawson Assoc, 1983, p 153.
147. Ames B: Dietary Carcinogens. *Science* 1983; 221:1256-1263.
148. Enig M, Munn R, Keeney M: Dietary fat and cancer trends: a critique. *Fed Proc* 1978; 37:2215-2220.
149. Hausman P: *Foods That Fight Cancer.* New York, Rawson Assoc, 1983, pp 118-119.
150. Drasar B, Irving D: Environmental factors and cancer of the colon and breast. *Br J Cancer* 1973; 27:167.
151. Hamilton E, Whitney E: *Understanding Nutrition,* ed 3. St. Paul, Minn, West Publishing Co, 1984, p 69.
152. Burkitt D: Epidemiology of large bowel disease: Role of fibre. *Proc Nutr Soc* 1973; 32:432.
153. McCormick D, Burns F, Albert R: Inhibition of benzopyrene-induced mammary carcinogenesis by retinyl acetate. *J Nat Canc Inst* 1981; 66:559-564.
154. Haydey R, Reed M, Czubox L, et al: Treatment of keratoacanthomas with oral 13-disretinoic acid. *N Eng J Med* 1980; 303:560-562.
155. Hirayama T: Diet and cancer. *Nutr Canc* 1979; 1:67-81.
156. Wald N, Idle M, Boreham J, et al: Low serum-vitamin-A and subsequent risk of cancer: Preliminary results of a prospective study. *Lancet* 1980; 2:813-815.
157. Kark J, Smith A, Switzer B, et al: Serum vitamin A (retinol) and cancer incidence in Evans County, Georgia. *J Nat Canc Inst* 1981; 66:7-16.
158. Hamilton E, Whitney E: *Understanding Nutrition,* ed 3. St. Paul, Minn, West Publishing Co, 1984, pp 295-297, 340, 435-436.
159. Medical News: Nitrosamines look more like human cancer villain. *JAMA* 1977; 238:15-20.

160. Hausman P: *Foods That Fight Cancer.* New York, Rawson Assoc, 1983, p 78.
161. Ibid, pp 96, 104, 138.
162. Ibid, pp 177-179.
163. Weinsier R: Overview: Salt and the development of essential hypertension. *Prev Med* 1976; 5:7.
164. Pagy L: Epidemiologic evidence on the etiology of human hypertension and its possible prevention. *Am Heart J* 1976; 91:527-534.
165. Dahl L: Effects of chronic excess salt ingestion. *Circ Res* 1968; 22:11.
166. McCarron D, Morris C, Cole C: Dietary calcium in human hypertension. *Science* 1982; 217:267.
167. McCarron D, Morris C, Henry K, et al: Blood pressure and nutrient intake in the United States. *Science* 1984; 224:1392-1398.
168. Resnick L, Nicholson J, Laragh J: Outpatient therapy of essential hypertension with dietary calcium supplementation. *J Am Col Card* 1984; 3:616.
169. Fernstrom J: Effects of the diet on brain neurotransmitters. *Metabolism* 1977; 26:207-223.
170. Zeisel S, Growden J: Diet and brain neurotransmitters. *Nutrition and the MD* 1980; 6:1.
171. Garrison R, Somer E: *The Nutrition Desk Reference.* New Canaan, Conn, Keats Publishing Co, 1985, p 222.
172. Holsboen F, Benkert O, Meier L, et al: Combined Estradiol and vitamin B_6 treatment in women with major depression. *Am J Psychi* 1985; 142:658.
173. Pollet P, Leathwood P: The influence of tryptophan on sleep in man. *Int J Vit Nutr Res* 1983; 53:223.
174. Egger J, Wilson J, Carter C, et al: Is migraine food allergy? A double-blind controlled trial of oligoantigenic diet treatment. *Lancet* 1983; 2:865-869.
175. Perkin J, Hartje J: Diet and migraine: A review of the literature. *J Am Diet Assoc* 1983; 83:459-463.
176. Chenault A: *Nutrition and Health.* New York, Holt Rinehart and Winston, 1984, pp 659, 664.
177. Hamilton E, Whitney E: *Understanding Nutrition,* ed 3. St. Paul, Minn, West Publishing Co, 1984, p 188.
178. Paffenbarger R, Hyde R: Exercise as protection against heart attack. *New Eng J Med* 1980; 302:1026.

179. Horowitz D: Diabetes and aging. *Am J Clin Nutr* 1982; 36:803-808.
180. Hamilton E, Whitney E: *Understanding Nutrition,* ed 3. St. Paul, Minn, West Publishing Co, 1984, p 46.

Additional Readings

Campbell N, Reade P, Radden B: Effect of cysteine on the survival of mice with transplanted malignant thymoma. *Nature* 1974; 251:158-159.

Hywyler T, Hirt A, Morell A: Effect of ascorbic acid on human natural killer cells. *Immun Let* 1985; 10:173-176.

Kent S: Rejuvenating the immune system. *Geriatrics* 1981; 36:13-22.

Shilotri P, Seetharam K: Effects of megadoses of vitamin C on bactericidal activity of leukocytes. *Am J Clin Nutr* 1977; 30:1077.

Glossary

Adrenal Gland: A ductless gland situated near the kidneys that produces and secretes several hormones including adrenalin and the corticosteroid hormone cortisone.

Amino Acid: A building block of protein; over 20 amino acids are used by the body to form proteins in hair, skin, blood, and other tissues.

Anemia: A reduction in the number, size, or color of red blood cells. Anemia results in reduced oxygen-carrying capacity of the blood.

Antibody: A substance in body fluids that is a component of the immune system and protects the body against disease and infection.

Antioxidant: A compound that protects other compounds or tissues from the destructive effects of oxygen derivatives.

Arrhythmia: Irregular heart beat.

Artery: A blood vessel that supplies blood, oxygen, and nutrients to the tissues.

Asthma: Shortness of breath, wheezing, and feelings of suffocation.

Bacteria: Microscopic one-celled organisms found in food, the body, and all living matter. Bacteria can contribute to both health and disease.

Caffeine: A drug that stimulates the nervous system and is found in coffee, some soft drinks, chocolate, tea, and some medications.

Calorie: A measurement of heat. In nutrition, calorie refers to the quantity of energy contained in foods.

Carbohydrate: The starches and sugars in the diet.

Carotene: The form of vitamin A found in plants.

Cholesterol: A type of fat found in foods from animal sources and produced by the body. High levels of cholesterol in the blood are associated with heart disease.

Cirrhosis: Inflammation or fatty infiltration of the liver.

Cruciferous: The group of vegetables called the "cabbage family" including cabbage, broccoli, asparagus, cauliflower, and kohlrabi. A diet high in these vegetables is associated with a reduced risk for cancer.

Diabetes: A disorder in which the body's ability to user sugar is impaired because of inadequate production or utilization of the hormone insulin.

Diuretic: An agent that increases the flow of urine.

Enzyme: A protein produced by the body that initiates and accelerates chemical reactions.

Endocrine Gland: Ductless glands that secrete hormones into the body that have profound effects on other organs and tissues. Examples of endocrine glands are ovaries, testes, thyroid, pancreas, and adrenal.

Free Radical: A highly reactive compound derived from air pollution, radiation, cigarette smoke, or the incomplete breakdown of proteins and fats. Free radicals react with fats in cell membranes and changes their shape or function.

Gastrointestinal: The stomach and intestinal tract.

Glucose: The building block of starch, sugar, and blood sugar.

Hematocrit: The volume percent of red blood cells in blood.

Hemoglobin: The oxygen-carrying protein in red blood cells.

Hepatitis: Inflammation of the liver.

Herpes: A skin disorder caused by a virus and characterized by pain and blisters.

High Density Lipoproteins (HDL): A substance comprised of fats and protein that serves as a transport vehicle for fats in the blood. A high level of HDL is associated with a reduced risk for cardiovascular disease.

Hormone: A chemical substance produced by a group of cells or an organ, called an endocrine gland, that is released into the blood and transported to another organ or tissue, where it performs a specific action. Examples of hormones are insulin, estrogen, testosterone, adrenalin.

Hypertension: High blood pressure.

Hydrogenated Fat: An unsaturated vegetable fat that has been processed to become more saturated, such as margarine and shortening.

Immune System: A complex system of interlocking substances and tissues that protects the body from disease.

Insulin: The hormone, secreted by the pancreas, that is responsible for the regulation of blood sugar.

Lethargy: Tired, sluggish, lack of energy.

Lymphocyte: A white blood cell that is a component of the immune system and aids in the protection of the body against disease and infection.

Metabolism: The sum total of all body processes, whereby the body converts foods into tissues and breaks down and repairs tissues and converts complex substances into simple ones for energy. Basal metabolism is the minimum amount of energy required to maintain body processes.

Migraine Headache: Intense pain in the head usually confined to one side of the head and sometimes followed by vomiting. Migraines often are preceded by changes in vision or other sensations.

Mucous Membranes: Linings of the throat, eyes, and other surfaces that secret a thick liquid that coats and protects the underlying tissues.

Obesity: Body weight more than 20% above desirable weight; excessive body fat.

Osteoporosis: Loss of calcium from the bone that results in reduced bone strength and increased fractures. Bones maintain the same diameter but become less dense.

Ozone: A highly reactive modification of oxygen whereby the two oxygen atoms in oxygen (O_2) are increased to three (O_3).

Pancreas: The organ responsible for the production and secretion of numerous digestive enzymes and the hormone insulin, which is responsible for the regulation of blood sugar (glucose).

Pectin: A water-soluble fiber found in fruits.

Platelets: Cell fragments in blood that aid in blood coagulation.

Saturated Fat: A type of fat that contains the maximum number of hydrogen atoms and is said to be "saturated" with hydrogen. Saturated fats are solid at room temperature and are found primarily in animal foods, margarine, shortening, and coconut and palm oil.

Serotonin: A hormone-like substances produced in the brain that regulates mood, sleep, and numerous other body processes.

Stressors: Anything that stimulates a person to react in a stressful manner.

Stress Hormones: The hormones produced and secreted by the adrenal glands. Stress hormones include cortisone and the corticosteroids, and epinephrin (adrenalin).

Tryptophan: An amino acid in the diet that the body uses to produce serotonin and niacin.

Type A Personality: A person who is aggressive, anxious, impatient, assumes high responsibility, works excessively, and is more prone to heart disease and stress than a type B personality.

Type B Personality: A person who is relaxed, not rushed, is not affected by deadlines or the demands of responsibililty, and who is less prone to heart attack and stress that a type A personality.

Tyramine: A compound in foods that might produce migraine headaches in some people.

Unsaturated Fat: A type of fat that has one or more spots where additional hydrogen could be added. Unsaturated fats are liquid at room temperature and are found primarily in vegetables and vegetable oils.

Virus: Any of a large group of minute particles that are capable of infecting plants, animals, and humans.

Vitamin: An essential nutrient required by the body in minute amounts and that must be obtained from foods.

Index